Sports and Activities

Let's Skateboard!

by Terri DeGezelle

Consulting Editor: Gail Saunders-Smith, PhD

Consultant: Kymm Ballard, MA
Physical Education, Athletics, and Sports Medicine Consultant
North Carolina Department of Public Instruction

Capstone
press

Mankato, Minnesota

Pebble Plus is published by Capstone Press,
151 Good Counsel Drive, P.O. Box 669, Mankato, Minnesota 56002.
www.capstonepress.com

1 2 3 4 5 6 11 10 09 08 07 06

Library of Congress Cataloging-in-Publication Data
DeGezelle, Terri, 1955-
   Let's skateboard! / by Terri DeGezelle.
   p. cm.—(Pebble plus. Sports and activities)
   Includes bibliographical references and index.
   ISBN-13: 978-0-7368-5365-1 (hardcover)
   ISBN-10: 0-7368-5365-0 (hardcover)
   1. Skateboarding—Juvenile literature. I. Title. II. Series.
GV859.8 .D44 2006
796.22—dc22
                                                        2005017942

Summary: Simple text and photographs present the skills, equipment, and safety concerns of skateboarding.

Editorial Credits
Heather Adamson, editor; Kia Adams, designer; Kelly Garvin, photo researcher

Photo Credits
Capstone Press/Gary Sundermeyer, 10–11; TJ Thoraldson Digital Photography, cover, 1, 8–9, 13, 16–17, 19, 21
Getty Images/The Image Bank/Benn Mitchell, 5; Mike Brinson, 6–7; Photographer's Choice/Joe McBride, 15

The author thanks Taylor Weness for sharing his knowledge of skateboarding.

Note to Parents and Teachers

The Sports and Activities set supports national physical education standards related
to recognizing movement forms and exhibiting a physically active lifestyle. This
book describes and illustrates skateboarding. The images support early readers in
understanding the text. The repetition of words and phrases helps early readers learn
new words. This book also introduces early readers to subject-specific vocabulary words,
which are defined in the Glossary section. Early readers may need assistance to read
some words and to use the Table of Contents, Glossary, Read More, Internet Sites, and
Index sections of the book.

Table of Contents

Skateboarding

Roll down the ramp.

Carve out a turn.

It's fun to skateboard!

Skateboarders can move
fast or slow.
They push one foot
on the ground
to move the board.

Skateboarders ride
on smooth surfaces.
They cruise over wood
and concrete.

Skateparks have slanted floors
and ramps for smooth riding.
Parks also have rails
and boxes for grinding.

Skateboarders do tricks.

They jump and spin.

They flip their boards

in the air.

Boards

Riders stand on a skateboard's flat deck. Trucks and wheels are bolted under the deck.

truck

deck

wheel

Skateboard Safety

Pads help keep skaters safe
from bumps and bruises.
Skateboarders wear helmets
to protect their heads.

Skateboarders take turns
skating down ramps.
They obey posted rules
and signs.

Having Fun

Let's grab a board
and roll fast.
Let's skateboard!

Glossary

carve—to lean a skateboard when turning so that the deck looks like a knife in a cutting position

deck—the flat, wooden part of a skateboard where riders stand

floor—the skateboard term for a skating surface

grinding—sliding on the underside of a skateboard deck instead of the wheels; skateboarders "grind" on railings, large boxes, and the edges of ramps.

helmet—a hard hat that protects the head

obey—to do what someone tells you to do

pad—a soft cushion of material

protect—to guard or keep safe

ramp—a slanted or U-shaped surface to roll down

truck—the parts of a skateboard that hold the wheels in place

Read More

Eckart, Edana. *I Can Skateboard.* Sports. New York: Children's Press, 2003.

Hughes, Morgan. *Skateboards.* Wheels in Motion. Vero Beach, Fla.: Rourke, 2004.

Klingel, Cynthia Fitterer, and Robert B. Noyed. *Skateboarding.* Wonder Books. Chanhassen, Minn.: Child's World, 2001.

Internet Sites

FactHound offers a safe, fun way to find Internet sites related to this book. All of the sites on FactHound have been researched by our staff.

Here's how:

1. Visit *www.facthound.com*

2. Type in this special code **0736853650** for age-appropriate sites. Or enter a search word related to this book for a more general search.

3. Click on the **Fetch It** button.

FactHound will fetch the best sites for you!

Index

Word Count: 123
Grade: 1
Early-Intervention Level: 13